THE BOOK OF

Numbers

ONE CHAPTER A DAY

GoodMorningGirls.org

The Book of Numbers

© 2015 Women Living Well Ministries, LLC

ALL RIGHTS RESERVED

Welcome to Good Morning Girls! We are so glad you are joining us.

God created us to walk with Him, to know Him, and to be loved by Him. He is our living well, and when we drink from the water He continually provides, His living water will change the entire course of our lives.

Jesus said: "Whoever drinks of the water that I will give him will never be thirsty again. The water that I will give him will become in him a spring of water welling up to eternal life." ~ John 4:14 (ESV)

So let's begin.

The method we use here at GMG is called the **SOAK** method.

- ❒ **S**—The S stands for *Scripture*—Read the chapter for the day. Then choose 1-2 verses and write them out word for word. (There is no right or wrong choice—just let the Holy Spirit guide you.)

- ❒ **O**—The O stands for *Observation*—Look at the verse or verses you wrote out. Write 1 or 2 observations. What stands out to you? What do you learn about the character of God from these verses? Is there a promise, command or teaching?

- ❒ **A**—The A stands for *Application*—Personalize the verses. What is God saying to you? How can you apply them to your life? Are there any changes you need to make or an action to take?

- ❒ **K**—The K stands for *Kneeling in Prayer*—Pause, kneel and pray. Confess any sin God has revealed to you today. Praise God for His word. Pray the passage over your own life or someone you love. Ask God to help you live out your applications.

SOAK God's word into your heart and squeeze every bit of nourishment you can out of each day's scripture reading. Soon you will find your life transformed by the renewing of your mind!

Walk with the King!

Courtney

WomenLivingWell.org, GoodMorningGirls.org

Join the GMG Community

Share your daily SOAK at 7:45am on **Facebook.com/GoodMorningGirlsWLW**

Instagram: WomenLivingWell #GoodMorningGirls

GMG Bible Coloring Chart

COLORS	KEYWORDS
PURPLE	God, Jesus, Holy Spirit, Saviour, Messiah
PINK	women of the Bible, family, marriage, parenting, friendship, relationships
RED	love, kindness, mercy, compassion, peace, grace
GREEN	faith, obedience, growth, fruit, salvation, fellowship, repentance
YELLOW	worship, prayer, praise, doctrine, angels, miracles,power of God, blessings
BLUE	wisdom, teaching, instruction, commands
ORANGE	prophecy, history, times, places, kings, genealogies, people, numbers, covenants, vows, visions, oaths, future
BROWN/GRAY	Satan, sin, death, hell, evil, idols, false teachers, hypocrisy, temptation

Introduction to the Book of Numbers

Whining and complaining is a misery to the ears that have to hear it. The book of Numbers records a story of unbelief—and God's unending patience with the Nation of Israel. Journey with us - and them—as we learn from Israel's mistakes. We may even recognize some of the same attitudes in our own lives.

Purpose: Numbers tells the story of how the nation of Israel prepared to enter into the Promised Land, how they were disobedient, and how they prepared to try again. Like the Nation of Israel, we are given second chances.

Author: Moses

Date: 1450-1410 BC

Setting: The Wildnerness of Sinai and the lands south and east of Canaan.

Key Verse: The Lord bless you and keep you; The Lord make his face to shine upon you and be gracious to you. (Numbers 6:24-25)

The book of Numbers begins with the children of Israel preparing for their journey to the Promised Land. They have received the law—and now a census must be taken. So, the people are counted (specifically, men for war). Then, the people are set apart for God and so, the journey begins.

With the beginning of the journey comes the beginning of the complaining. From food to leadership, the people are unhappy. They arrive at Kadesh, and the twelve spies are sent in. Ten come out with fear. Two, Joshua and Caleb, come out ready to do battle and possess what God has already given to them. Unbelief strikes the camp—and because of their unbelief, the current generation will not go into the Promised Land- and the wandering begins.

The ending is similar to the beginning. A new generation is preparing to go into the land. They are set apart and numbered.

A Layout of the Book:

1. Preparation for the Journey (1:1-10:10)

The census is taken, the Levities are given their roll, the camp is purified and they receive instructions for their journey. The topic of purity comes up (similar to Leviticus) as God wants to be sure His people are set apart as they enter the nations around them. He desires them to be holy—a people set apart for Him. Our application is how should we, as the church, be a set apart people for Him?

2. The First Journey to the Promised Land (10:11-14:45)

As the people journey to the Promised Land—they begin to complain. As the 12 spies enter- 10 come out with unbelief, and 2 come out full of faith. For our application, we can think about our attitude over the state that God has us in. We can also look at our faith—is God asking us to do something we feel is too big for us? Are we looking at life through eyes of faith or fear? When we walk without faith, we are robbing ourselves of the blessings of God.

3. Wandering (15:1-21:35)

There was punishment for their discontentment and lack of faith. We see this over and over in the chapters that are in this section. When we struggle with discontentment and disobedience, there is always a consequence for our actions. Are there areas in our lives that we need to evaluate?

4. Approaching the Promise Land for the Second Time (22:1-36:13)

Here we will find the story of Balaam—who falls into temptation. He knew what was right, and sinned anyway. We need to be careful that we don't just have head knowledge, but that we live out our faith.

Throughout the book of Numbers, we see wandering and rebellion. We'll be forced to take a deeper look at our own faith. Are we in a place of wandering—a place where we are stuck because we won't live out our faith?

The book of Numbers is going to ask us to walk along Israel, to learn from their mistakes, and to see our patient God of second chances as we head to the Promised Land of the abundant Christian life.

The Lord spoke to Moses...

Take a census...according to the number

of names, every male, head by head.

From twenty years old and upward

who are able to go to war.

Numbers 1:1~3

Reflection Question:

The Levities were given a specific calling to care for the tabernacle.

God gives each of us a specific calling as well. What has He called you to do for Him?

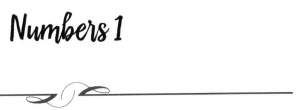

S—The S stands for *Scripture*

O—The O stands for *Observation*

A—The A stands for *Application*

K—The K stands for *Kneeling in Prayer*

They shall camp facing the

tent of meeting on every side.

Numbers 2:2

Reflection Question:

The children of Israel obeyed what the Lord said. They followed his direction, even with where to sleep!

What direction has God given you that may not seem important or make sense right now but you must follow?

Numbers 2

S—The S stands for *Scripture*

O—The O stands for *Observation*

A—The A stands for *Application*

K—The K stands for *Kneeling in Prayer*

I consecrated for my own all

the firstborn in Israel,

both of man and of beast.

They shall be mine: I am the Lord.

Numbers 3:13

Reflection Question:

God gave specific instructions throughout His Word that must be obeyed. If we are not obedient there will be consequences.

How have you know this to be true in your life?

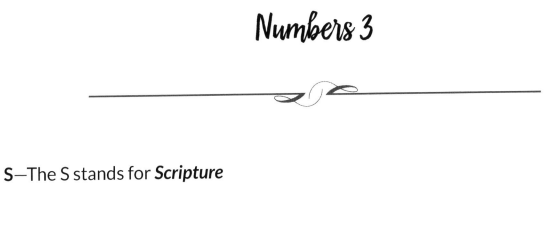

Numbers 3

S—The S stands for *Scripture*

O—The O stands for *Observation*

A—The A stands for *Application*

K—The K stands for *Kneeling in Prayer*

They shall not go in
to look on the holy things
even for a moment,
lest they die.

Numbers 4:20

Reflection Question:

Sometimes the tasks God calls us to are a burden. They can be difficult to bear.

How have you been obedient to God when the task seemed like too much of a burden to carry?

S—The S stands for *Scripture*

O—The O stands for *Observation*

A—The A stands for *Application*

K—The K stands for *Kneeling in Prayer*

He shall confess his sin

that he has committed.

And he shall make full

restitution for his wrong.

Numbers 5:7

Reflection Question:

Sin is always found out, for we cannot hide anything from God. We must confess our sins to the Lord in order to keep our relationship with Him growing.

What is hindering you from drawing near to Him today?

S—The S stands for *Scripture*

O—The O stands for *Observation*

A—The A stands for *Application*

K—The K stands for *Kneeling in Prayer*

The Lord bless you and keep you;

The Lord make his face to shine

upon you and be gracious to you.

Numbers 6:24~25

Reflection Question:

The Lord desires to bless His people.

What blessings have clearly been given to you from God?

S—The S stands for *Scripture*

O—The O stands for *Observation*

A—The A stands for *Application*

K—The K stands for *Kneeling in Prayer*

When Moses went into the tent of meeting to speak with the Lord, he heard the voice speaking to him from above the mercy seat that was on the ark of the testimony.

Numbers 7:89

Reflection Question:

God asks every child of His to keep Him first, to obey Him above all and to give Him the honor and glory due to Him.

How does this truth help you in your personal Christian walk?

Numbers 7

S—The S stands for **Scripture**

O—The O stands for **Observation**

A—The A stands for **Application**

K—The K stands for **Kneeling in Prayer**

The Lord spoke to Moses, saying,

"Take the Levites from among the people

of Israel and cleanse them."

Numbers 8:4

Reflection Question:

All that belongs to God must be set apart and cleansed. Jesus' blood cleanses us, but we must ensure that we remain set apart throughout our daily lives.

What steps do you take to ensure that you remain set apart from the world?

Numbers 8

S—The S stands for *Scripture*

O—The O stands for *Observation*

A—The A stands for *Application*

K—The K stands for *Kneeling in Prayer*

At the command of the Lord they camped, and at the command of the Lord they set out.

Numbers 9:23

Reflection Question:

The people of Israel faithfully followed God's guidance.

How are you following God's guidance in your life right now?

Numbers 9

S—The S stands for *Scripture*

O—The O stands for *Observation*

A—The A stands for *Application*

K—The K stands for *Kneeling in Prayer*

Arise, O Lord,

and let your enemies

be scattered.

Numbers 10:34,35

Reflection Question:

Familiar places and things often call to us when God desires us to follow Him to the unknown.

Where has God asked you to follow Him that was unknown to you at the time?

S—The S stands for **Scripture**

O—The O stands for **Observation**

A—The A stands for **Application**

K—The K stands for **Kneeling in Prayer**

The people complained in the hearing of the Lord about their misfortunes, and when the Lord heard it, His anger was kindled, and the fire of the Lord burned among them and consumed some outlying parts of the camp.

Numbers 11:1

Reflection Question:

God takes care of His children's needs, yet if we're not careful we can grow weary of His provision and long for something different...something more.

How do you ensure that your spirit remains grateful for His provision?

S—The S stands for *Scripture*

O—The O stands for *Observation*

A—The A stands for *Application*

K—The K stands for *Kneeling in Prayer*

Now the man Moses was very meek,

more than all people who

were on the face of the earth.

Numbers 12:3

Reflection Question:

Moses was a meek man and though his siblings had spoken against him, he asked God to heal Miriam. He offered forgiveness without being asked.

Who can you give the gift of forgiveness to, though they haven't asked?

S—The S stands for *Scripture*

O—The O stands for *Observation*

A—The A stands for *Application*

K—The K stands for *Kneeling in Prayer*

Caleb quieted the people before Moses and said,

"Let us go up at once and occupy it,

for we are well able to overcome it."

Numbers 13:30

Reflection Question:

Even though the land of Canaan was promised to them and God had provided for them, the people still did not trust God to bring them into the Promised Land safely.

What is God asking you to trust Him to do today?

Numbers 13

S—The S stands for **Scripture**

O—The O stands for **Observation**

A—The A stands for **Application**

K—The K stands for **Kneeling in Prayer**

The Lord is with us

do not fear them.

Numbers 14:9

Reflection Question:

When we fail to take God at His word and seek to do things our own way, He will allow us to wander. In the midst of our wanderings we often miss out on the blessings God has for us.

What blessings have you missed out on because of your own wanderings?

Numbers 14

S—The S stands for *Scripture*

O—The O stands for *Observation*

A—The A stands for *Application*

K—The K stands for *Kneeling in Prayer*

Remember and do

all my commandments,

and be holy to your God.

Numbers 15:40

Reflection Question:

God wants to be remembered by His children. He desires that we follow His instructions to deepen our relationship with Him.

How do you ensure that you remember God throughout each day?

S—The S stands for *Scripture*

O—The O stands for *Observation*

A—The A stands for *Application*

K—The K stands for *Kneeling in Prayer*

All the congregation of the people of Israel grumbled against Moses and against Aaron and the Lord spoke to Moses, saying "Get away from the midst of this congregation, that I may consume them in a moment." And they fell on their faces.

Numbers 16:41, 44 & 45

Reflection Question:

Humility is an important part of a Christian's life. We must remember that it is God who works through us. We are nothing without Him.

What has God done in or through you that was clearly the work of His holy hands?

Numbers 16

S—The S stands for *Scripture*

O—The O stands for *Observation*

A—The A stands for *Application*

K—The K stands for *Kneeling in Prayer*

I will make to cease from me

the grumblings of the people of Israel.

Numbers 17:5

Reflection Question:

God showed that he did not tolerate the grumbling of the people through the sign of the budding staff.

In what area of your life do you struggle with grumbling?

Numbers 17

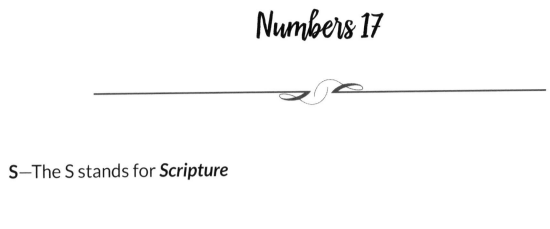

S—The S stands for *Scripture*

O—The O stands for *Observation*

A—The A stands for *Application*

K—The K stands for *Kneeling in Prayer*

I am your portion

and your inheritance

among the people of Israel.

Numbers 18:20

Reflection Question:

God provides for every need to those who serve Him. If He is calling you to do something, it is important that you not let doubt of His provision keep you from obeying Him.

When you've obeyed God, how have you seen Him provide for you?

Numbers 18

S—The S stands for **Scripture**

O—The O stands for **Observation**

A—The A stands for **Application**

K—The K stands for **Kneeling in Prayer**

If a man who is unclean

does not cleanse himself,

that person shall be cut off

from the midst of the assembly.

Numbers 19:20

Reflection Question:

The people were told to cleanse themselves from anything unclean. Jesus cleanses us from all of our impurities and sins.

How does remembering that we've been cleansed by the blood of the lamb change how you will live today?

S—The S stands for *Scripture*

O—The O stands for *Observation*

A—The A stands for *Application*

K—The K stands for *Kneeling in Prayer*

These are the waters of Meribah, where the people of Israel quarreled with the Lord, and through them he showed himself holy.

Numbers 20:13

Reflection Question:

Instead of focusing on all the great things God had done for them, the people continued to complain.

What are some things you can praise God for today?

S—The S stands for **Scripture**

O—The O stands for **Observation**

A—The A stands for **Application**

K—The K stands for **Kneeling in Prayer**

The people came to Moses and said,

"We have sinned, for we have

spoken against the Lord and you."

Numbers 21:13

Reflection Question:

As punishment for their discontentment, God sent serpents. Those who were bitten could be saved by fixing their eyes on a bronze serpent.

How does this remind you to keep your eyes fixed on Jesus?

Numbers 21

S—The S stands for *Scripture*

O—The O stands for *Observation*

A—The A stands for *Application*

K—The K stands for *Kneeling in Prayer*

Then Balaam said to the angel of the Lord,

"I have sinned, for I did not know that

you stood in the road against me."

Numbers 22:34

Reflection Question:

Balaam became displeased with his donkey because it would not move, only to find out that it wasn't moving because of God's angel.

Name a time that you became angry because things were not working out the way you wanted them to, only to discover that it was God's plan for things to not work out.

S—The S stands for *Scripture*

O—The O stands for *Observation*

A—The A stands for *Application*

K—The K stands for *Kneeling in Prayer*

God is not man, that he should lie, or a son of man,

that he should change his mind.

Has he said and will he not do it?

Or has he spoken, and will he not fulfill it?

Numbers 23:19

Reflection Question:

Balak sought to have God curse His people, which caused him to be cursed instead.

How can this bring you comfort today?

S—The S stands for *Scripture*

O—The O stands for *Observation*

A—The A stands for *Application*

K—The K stands for *Kneeling in Prayer*

Blessed are those who bless you,

And cursed are those who curse you.

Numbers 24:16

Reflection Question:

Balaam was able to foresee the future of God's people even though he was wicked. Many see the works of God but only a few truly believe.

Is there someone in your life who this holds true for? Let's pray for them today.

S—The S stands for *Scripture*

O—The O stands for *Observation*

A—The A stands for *Application*

K—The K stands for *Kneeling in Prayer*

The people ate and bowed down

To their gods

And the anger of the Lord

was kindled against Israel.

Numbers 25:2,3

Reflection Question:

Today we see the importance of those we surround ourselves with.

How do you ensure you have great quality friendships in your life? What qualities do you look for in that person?

Numbers 25

S—The S stands for *Scripture*

O—The O stands for *Observation*

A—The A stands for *Application*

K—The K stands for *Kneeling in Prayer*

The Lord said to Moses,

"Take a census of all the congregation of Israel, from

twenty years old and upward by their fathers' houses,

all in Israel who are able to go to war."

Numbers 26:2

Reflection Question:

In Numbers 26:63-65 we are reminded that God remains faithful to His word and judgments.

How does this bring you comfort?

S—The S stands for *Scripture*

O—The O stands for *Observation*

A—The A stands for *Application*

K—The K stands for *Kneeling in Prayer*

So the Lord said to Moses,

"Take Joshua the son of Nun,

a man in whom is the Spirit,

and lay your hand on him."

Numbers 27:18

Reflection Question:

Today we read that Joshua is the one who has been chosen to lead the people into the Promised Land.

What were the traits that made Joshua qualified for this responsibility (look back at Numbers 14:5-10)?

S—The S stands for *Scripture*

O—The O stands for *Observation*

A—The A stands for *Application*

K—The K stands for *Kneeling in Prayer*

You shall offer a burnt offering to the Lord:

two bulls from the herd,

one ram, and seven male lambs

a year old without blemish.

Numbers 28:11

Reflection Question:

In today's reading, the people of Israel are reminded of the sacrifices and offerings they are to bring to the Lord.

As Christians, why is it important to be reminded of the ultimate sacrifice that was made freely for us?

S—The S stands for *Scripture*

O—The O stands for *Observation*

A—The A stands for *Application*

K—The K stands for *Kneeling in Prayer*

You shall have a holy convocation.

You shall not do any ordinary work.

Numbers 29:1

Reflection Question:

Daily the people were to offer sacrifices; however, there were times when they were to stop from all activities and focus solely on God.

How does applying this same practice help you spiritually?

S—The S stands for *Scripture*

O—The O stands for *Observation*

A—The A stands for *Application*

K—The K stands for *Kneeling in Prayer*

If a man vows a vow to the Lord,

or swears an oath to bind himself by a pledge,

he shall not break his word.

Numbers 30:2

Reflection Question:

Today we learned the importance of making and keeping the vows we make to God.

How do you remain faithful to your word to God?

S—The S stands for **Scripture**

O—The O stands for **Observation**

A—The A stands for **Application**

K—The K stands for **Kneeling in Prayer**

Purify yourselves.

Numbers 31:19

Reflection Question:

God gave specific instructions for how the Israelites were to handle the plunder from war. The purpose was to preserve the holiness of God's people.

How are you careful to not allow the things of this world to drag you away from holiness?

Numbers 31

S—The S stands for *Scripture*

O—The O stands for *Observation*

A—The A stands for *Application*

K—The K stands for *Kneeling in Prayer*

Be sure your sin

will find you out.

Numbers 32:23

Reflection Question:

The people of Gad and the people of Reuben decided they did not want to receive their inheritance in the Promised Land. Instead, they preferred to receive it on their current side of the Jordan River.

Share a time when you allowed fear, comfort or worldly desires to hold you back from what God had planned for you.

Numbers 32

―――――――――――――― ⌘ ――――――――――――――

S—The S stands for *Scripture*

O—The O stands for *Observation*

A—The A stands for *Application*

K—The K stands for *Kneeling in Prayer*

You shall take possession of

the land and settle in it,

For I have given the land to you

To possess it.

Numbers 33:53

Reflection Question:

The Israelites were told to remove all the idolaters and their idols so that they themselves would not fall into temptation.

Are there things that God is laying on your heart that you need to separate yourself from?

Numbers 33

S—The S stands for **Scripture**

O—The O stands for **Observation**

A—The A stands for **Application**

K—The K stands for **Kneeling in Prayer**

You shall take one chief

from every tribe

to divide the land for inheritance.

Numbers 34:18

Reflection Question:

The land was very fruitful and could supply all of the people's needs. God once again provided them with everything they needed.

How has God met your needs recently?

S—The S stands for *Scripture*

O—The O stands for *Observation*

A—The A stands for *Application*

K—The K stands for *Kneeling in Prayer*

For I the Lord dwell

in the midst of the

people of Israel.

Numbers 35:34

Reflection Question:

God provided a refuge for those who committed murder until they could be judged appropriately. Jesus is our refuge.

How does knowing this bring you encouragement and comfort today?

S—The S stands for *Scripture*

O—The O stands for *Observation*

A—The A stands for *Application*

K—The K stands for *Kneeling in Prayer*

These are the commandments and the rules that the Lord commanded through Moses to the people of Israel.

Numbers 36:13

Reflection Question:

God commanded that marriages take place within their own tribes in order to protect their inheritance. There is a sure inheritance waiting for those who have placed their faith in Jesus, in heaven.

How does knowing that a glorious inheritance waits for you change the way you live today?

S—The S stands for *Scripture*

O—The O stands for *Observation*

A—The A stands for *Application*

K—The K stands for *Kneeling in Prayer*

Special Thanks

I want to extend a special thank you to Mandy Kelly, Rosilind Jukic, Bridget Childress and Misty Leask for your help with this journal. Your love, dedication and leadership to the Good Morning Girls ministry is such a blessing to all. Thank you for giving to the Lord.

~ Courtney

Made in the USA
San Bernardino, CA
24 May 2016